NAVAJO SANDPAINTING ART

EUGENE BAATSOSLANII JOE   MARK BAHTI

Photography by:

OSCAR T. BRANSON

Eugene Baatsoslanii Joe was born in Shiprock, New Mexico and raised near Sheep Springs, New Mexico. Descended from a long line of Navajo medicine men, including the famous Hosteen Klah, Eugene began receiving formal instruction in Navajo sandpainting and religion at age 10 from his father, James C. Joe. Though he has never received any art training in school, he has developed his own unique style and become widely recognized as an outstanding young artist, having taken many awards for his work since he first entered competition in 1968.

Mark Bahti has been involved in Indian art for a number of years, currently operating an Indian art shop in Tucson, Arizona that was started by his father the late Tom Bahti, over a quarter of a century ago. Like his father before him, he has written and lectured widely on Indian cultures and their crafts and has been active not simply in organizations concerned with Indian art, but also with those Indian organizations that seek to improve the welfare of the Indians through self-help programs.

Oscar Branson has been active in the Indian and Primitive Art fields for much of his lifetime. The successful operation of the Primitive Arts Store, The Treasure Chest in Santa Fe, New Mexico, gave him the opportunity to write and publish the best selling books including: *Turquoise The Gem Of The Centuries — Fetishes And Carvings Of The Southwest and Indian Jewelry Making*. The opportunity to join the authors by doing the photography for *Navajo Sandpainting Art* has been most gratifying.

Printed by

WALSWORTH
PUBLISHING
COMPANY
MARCELINE, MISSOURI 64658

FOREWORD

While we hope to give the reader a general understanding and appreciation of Navajo religion, it will be only as it relates to Navajo sandpainting art.

Navajo sandpainting art is based upon traditional Navajo sandpainting and the rich lore of Navajo religion, but is different in intent and increasingly different in appearance. While generally regarded as being primarily decorative in nature, it is now becoming an important media for the Navajo artist who wishes to symbolically interpret his expression of his heritage and his feelings. In the legendary past, when the *Dinneh** were first taught these sandpaintings and the ceremonies that go with them, the *Deginneh*, or Holy People, warned against the disastrous consequences if the ceremonial knowledge was not kept alive. The *Dinneh* promised to protect and revere this knowledge. We feel that *Navajo Sandpainting Art* can help keep that promise.

*The Navajo called themselves *"Dinneh"*, meaning "the People".

ACKNOWLEDGEMENTS

We wish to acknowledge the assistance given us by many people, including Herbert Beenhouwer, Nelson Begay, Ethel Branson, Ed Foutz, Jack Fowler, James C. Joe, Russ Lingruen, Scott Ryerson, John Tanner, Amber Wolcott and Tom Wheeler.

Speial recognition is due those who came before us, such as father Berard Haile, Hosteen Klah, L.C. Wyman, Slim Curly, Gladys Reichard, Miguelito and others who had the foresight to help preserve Navajo ceremonial knowledge for future generations.

Eugene Joe would also like to express his appreciation for the encouragement in his work from Will Sampson, Robert Redford, Rita Coolidge, Kris Kristofferson, Gene Cotton and Ernest Borgnine, with deepest, special thanks to Glenna Washburn and to his father James C. Joe.

DEDICATION

To our fathers, in grateful appreciation for all they have shared with us.

INTRODUCTION

According to Navajo religion, the Universe is a very delicately balanced thing, full of enormously powerful forces, with potential for good or evil. If this balance is upset, even unintentionally, some disaster - usually an illness - will result. Further, it is believed that only Man can upset the balance.

To restore the balance or harmony means performing one of the myriad Navajo Chants or Ways. These are long and complex ceremonies that may last from one to nine days. Involving the use of medicinal herbs, prayers, sandpaintings and songs, these Ways recount a portion of Navajo legendary history that relates to the particular illness and its cause. By ceremonially identifying with the hero of the myth in his eventual triumph, the patient becomes stronger and harmony is restored, thereby effecting a cure.

The scene is as ancient as the Navajo people The setting is the traditional Navajo hogan, with Mother Earth for a floor and the entrance facing east. The elders of the tribe, in sitting cross-legged, awaken the silence with the shaking of gourd rattles and the chanting begins.

The sunstreams in through the smokehole of the hogan, bathing the patient in its light. The chanting continues, unfolding the exploits of one of the heroes of Navajo legend.

The sandpainting is done in a careful and sacred manner, according to the ancient knowledge of the art, with each figure, and each design in order and done with the five sacred colors.

As the patient is seated atop the completed sandpainting, the *hatathli* (medicine man) bends to reverently touch a portion of a figure in the sandpainting, then moves to touch the patient, transferring the medicine and the power. As this is done, the sickness falls from the patient and harmony returns.

Then, before the sun sets, the sandpainting is erased with a sacred feather staff and is swept onto a blanket to be carried outside and carefully disposed of. In casting it away, the last of the sickness is carried away from the patient, who, healed through faith, rises to walk in beauty once again.

Care must be taken to perform the ceremony correctly, down to the smallest detail, lest disaster befall all present. A medicine man's apprentice will spend years learning a single Way before ever performing it himself. (Navajo society is a matriarchal one, but even so, few women ever become a *hatathli*.)

The importance of these ceremonies to the Navajo should not be underestimated or demeaned. Over the last two decades a number of doctors and hospitals serving the Navajo have come to realize that to successfully treat a Navajo patient it is often necessary to do it in conjunction with a *hatathli*.

Most ethnologists feel that the Navajo probably learned sandpainting from the Pueblo Indians who, fearing reprisals from the Spanish after the Great Pueblo Revolt of 1680, went to live among the Navajo. Since that time sandpaintings have declined somewhat in importance among the Pueblo Indians, but have been refined and evolved onto a vastly more complex level among the Navajo, for whom it plays a major role in their religion.

According to Navajo history, however, the *Dinneh* were first shown the art of sandpainting as part of their ceremonial instruction from the Holy Ones, who were never seen by human eyes. Instead they became known only through the instructions they relayed through the spirits, such as the Wind People, who passed on knowledge of the ceremonial songs to the Navajo.

Among the sacred knowledge given the first apprentices, during the seven days and seven nights of their purification and instruction, were songs, prayers and sandpaintings, as well as medicine tools — objects and plants with protective or curative powers.

The ceremonial paintings which were revealed to them were painted on scrolls made of Mountain Sheep skin, but they were told they must do the sandpaintings with sand, on Mother Earth, to prevent the knowledge from being hoarded and to insure that anyone with the necessary ability and patience might learn them. As the Holy People told them:

> We will not give you this picture;
> Men are not as good as we;
> They might quarrel over the picture and tear it
> and that would bring misfortune;
> The black cloud would not come again,
> and the rain would not fall;
> the corn would not grow.
> But you may paint it on the ground,
> with the colors of the earth.

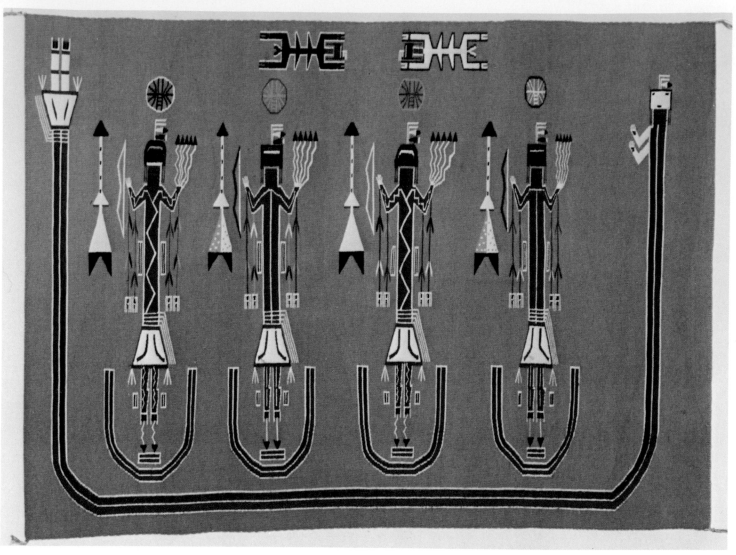

An excellent example of a Navajo rug with a sandpainting design, often erroneously called a "ceremonial rug", it is never used in any ceremony.

One of the first recorded instances where traditional Navajo sandpainting designs were used in a non-traditional manner took place in the late 1890's near Shiprock. It was here that a Navajo woman came to the trading post with a rug unlike anything the trader had ever seen—it had the figure of *yei-bih-chai* dancer woven into it.

The trader, perhaps thinking to encourage more of these, displayed it prominently in his post. The Navajo in the area were equally—if unfavorably—surprised by the rug. Word travelled quickly and soon a delegation of Navajo, including at least one *hatathli*, arrived to inform the trader that he must remove the offending rug from sight immediately. He did so, selling it not long after to a collector from the East for a considerable sum of money.

Though both the weaver and the trader were thoroughly chastised, the premium price paid for the rug brought about economic pressures that eventually relaxed the strict taboo against weaving *yei* rugs, as they came to be called. Even a Navajo *hatathli*, Hosteen Klah, wove a number of rugs of nearly complete sandpainting designs in his attempts to help record some of the vanishing ceremonial knowledge. Even so, most medicine men still disapprove of them, though they do not actively discourage them any longer.

For the next half century, until the late 1940's the only reproductions of sandpaintings that appeared anywhere else were usually done in association with efforts to record Navajo ceremonial knowledge. Some were done by Anglo ethnologists and traders, others by the Navajo, but most were watercolor or colored pencil on paper.

A few of the hotels that served the tourists who visited the Southwest on the Santa Fe Railroad had sandpaintings done with oil paints on the walls of their great lobbies, and a few were done on stuccoed boards, but none were done with sand.

The breakthrough came about 1947 and is often attributed to David Villasenor, a man from Mexico who worked for a period of time with Gladys Reichard, who was a friend of the Navajo who sought to preserve those ceremonies that were in danger of being lost.

Up until this time attempts to make permanent sandpaintings were restricted to doing them in the traditional fashion and, after it was completed, trying to stabilize it. Villasenor decided it was far more logical to concentrate on the stabilizing from the beginning. In 1949 he developed the How-To-Do-Sandpainting kit which even some Navajo used in their first attempts.

THE NEW ART IS PASSED ON

The first Navajo to do this new type of sandpainting was Fred Stevens, also known as Grey Squirrel. He then taught Frances Miller of Sheep Springs, an area where most of the sandpaintings artists are from, even to the present day.

The Joe family, which includes a number of sand-painters among them, is a good example of how the art of sandpainting is being taught and passed down.

James C. Joe, the patriarch of the family, first began learning traditional sandpainting at age 10, from his grandfather, who instructed him in the Navajo religion. Joe later became a medicine man, the only sandpainter to have been one. His aunt, the wife of Frances Miller, introduced Joe to sandpainting on boards in 1962. Joe went on to experiment with the new media, making other improvements and developing his own techniques. As a former medicine man his knowledge and respect for his peoples' beliefs are evident in his work, work whose beauty reveals the patience and perseverance which marks a true artist. It is his belief that only an original sandpainting will expose the art as a masterpiece, for in it the artist who demonstrates the knowledge gained in years of apprenticeship in the ancient religion and its art.

Joe has passed this knowledge on to many members of his family, including one of his sons, Eugene, who describes how he learned the art and developed his own style in the following account:

"The first stage of my education in sandpainting came from amusing myself, as a young child, with drawing. My tools were my fingers and the drawing surface was the desert sand covering of Mother Earth. I had the glorious light from Father Sky to light my childish artistic attempts. Subject matter was no problem as there was the world of nature surrounding me to select from.

This carving by Navajo artist Tom Yazzie shows how the Navajo Yei-bih-chai dancers look. This figure represents B'ganaskiddy.

Painted by Nelson Begay, this shows a Navajo chanter or Hatathli performing the Shooting Chant for a patient.

My father perceived my interest and thus began my formal instruction in tratitional sandpainting under his patient tutelage. At first my tasks were menial: grinding the rocks of various colors, keeping the workshop clean and preparing the boards for the paintings he did. Like most apprentices, I found the work tedious, but I quickly learned that they are a very necessary part of the whole procedure and would result in a beautiful creation. All forms of art demand discipline if pride of good craftsmanship is to be developed and sandpainting is no exception.

Of course, physical labor was only one element of my instruction. I would carefully listen to my father's spiritual instruction, which was the most essential element. He instilled in me the feelings of reverence, pride and beauty in the traditional Navajo sandpainting.

I worked under my father's guidance for 12 years. As I became older I sought out others, particularly artists (not exclusively Indian), who were willing to share their ideas and knowledge in order to enrich my training. My quest seemed insatiable: as I began to ally myself with these people I found myself yearning to learn ever more. My friends were generous with their time and talents and I shall forever be indebted to them.

My greatest desire is to preserve this traditional native craft with all the reverence and respect it deserves, indeed, demands, but also to present it in a manner for all who see my work to receive pleasure from it. I owe this sense of dedication to my father, my family, my people, my friends."

Illustrated here are some of the rocks from which Navajo grind their sand. Five basic colors are used; white, black, blue, yellow and red. Some sandpainters obtain their colors from rocks which are slightly radioactive or from minerals which fluoresce, making photographing sandpaintings, in which such materials were used, very challenging.

CREATING A SANDPAINTING

Sandpainting can be tedious, exacting work, requiring a great deal of preparation before the actual painting can begin. As with most arts or crafts, the more time spent at it and the more patient and demanding the artisan, the better the final result.

First the rock must be collected; rock, which according to the *Yo-he* or Bead Chant, are the fragments left from the defeat of the Rock People. Most of the rock used is gathered within the traditional (as opposed to the modern legal) boundaries of the Navajo Reservation. Most sandpainters keep the locations where they obtain their rock a closely guarded secret.

In the last two or three years a few individuals have begun using commercially-colored sands or coloring neutral sand themselves, using oil pigments. Currently the colors are not too dificult for the untrained eye to spot as they have a bright glossy appearance.

After the rock has been sledgehammered loose it is stored in buckets for the journey home. It is then broken up into still smaller pieces and allowed to completely dry before being ground, using a *mano and metate*, mortar and pestle or, more recently, a hand-operated coffee-grinder. The drying is important, for the true color of a stone is not revealed until all the moisture is gone.

When it has been ground the sand is sifted and strained into three grades of fineness. Dust or powdered stone is avoided as it is very difficult to control when used for sandpainting.

Sheets of ½ inch or ⅜ inch particle board or plywood are sawed into the desired sizes and shapes and the edges are sanded smooth. Then glue is spread evenly over the entire surface to insure that the sand will adhere smoothly and evenly. The glue used by each artist varies. Basically it is thinned white household glue, but most add other ingredients and the formulas are kept secret.

The boards are then placed outside in the sun for up to several days to allow them to completely dry. Afterwards the surface may be lightly sanded to remove any buildups and insure a smooth working surface.

Then the actual painting begins. Using fine brushes, the design is applied in glue. To prevent the glue from drying before the sand is applied only one section is done at a time and to prevent the mixing of colors only one color of sand is used each time.

A second color or second section is not begun until the artist is satisfied the first has completely dried. A careful artist may spend several weeks working on a large sandpainting with many shades of color.

The method of applying the sand varies, with each artist having developed his or her own technique. The most common method is to place a pinch of sand in the palm just beneath the second finger and allow it to trickle out from the index finger, using the thumb to regulate the flow. The flow must be soft and even or the line will be distorted and indistinct. If too much glue has been used there will be a high build-up of sand and if too little was used the line will be faint and indistinct.

While some sandpainters may actually pencil in the figure they plan to make, most will make only a few measurements or marks to insure symmetry. Still others, with far greater skill and practice, work almost entirely by eye.

When the sandpainting has been completed it is allowed to dry for a day or two more. Then the entire surface will be lightly sprayed with a fine mist of shellac to make sure the sand on the very surface is secure. Care must be taken to prevent buildups, of shellac which occur as glossy areas that cannot be successfully removed.

Southern Utah, where Navajo sandpainters obtain many of the rocks which they grind into sand for their sandpaintings.

PERSPECTIVES

It should be noted that because of the different cultural perspectives, what appears to be a variation in a sandpainting to a non-Navajo, may not be to a Navajo. As an example, a *yei* may have a blue *or* a green face. To the Navajo both colors are correct because, in the ceremonial manner of classifying color, they are not two, but one color. The Navajo recognize blue and green turquoise as being different, but since blue and green have the same purpose in sandpaintings, they are thought of as being the same.

Another example of the difference in the way of looking at something is kinship and identity. Monster Slayer, one of the Twin War Gods, is often identified as Holy Man, Changing Woman's child and her grandchild as well. All are the same, but since they each emphasize a certain part of the personality of Monster Slayer, they are not entirely the same. To a Navajo it is no more confusing than a woman being a sister, grandmother, daughter and mother at the same time.

In a chant, such as one from the Creation Myth, the opening lines of a song are; Monster Slayer, you are his child, he is your child/First Man, you are his child, he is your child/Born-of-Water, you are his child, he is your child/First Woman, you are her child, she is your child. . . ." There is no contradiction here either since the purpose is to stress the symbolic identification with these powerful personages in order to effect a cure for the patient.

It is impossible for a non-Navajo to truly be able to view things through Navajo eyes, but by being aware of some of the differences in the manner of viewing things, it can be compensated for to some degree. By making an earnest attempt to do so, one cannot only better understand and respect Navajo sandpaintings, but also Navajo culture itself.

MALE AND FEMALE YEIS

The *Yeis* are supernatural beings from Navajo religion, with the word *'yei'* being usually translated as 'god'. The masked dancers who portray the *Yei* in certain ceremonies are referred to as *Yei-bih-chai-* dancers, after the *Yei-bih-chai* ceremony in which they appear.

Although there are exceptions to the rule, a round head indicates a male *Yei* and a square or slightly rectangular head indicates a female *Yei*. The male *Yei* in this sandpainting should not have the two feathers on the side of his head.

He is holding a rattle and crooked lightning while she is holding a rattle and evergreen. Hanging from their wrists and elbows are ribbons. Both should be holding rattles in their right hands and evergreen in their left. The skirt or kilt and the bag to the left of each *Yei* are the only two areas in traditional sandpainting where the sandpainter is permitted to vary the design.

Errors or variations not accepted in traditional sandpaintings appear in this type of sandpainting, almost regularly, especially in the larger ones. Knowledgeable Navajo sandpainters will often deliberately put in an "error" to prevent the sandpainting from exactly copying a ceremonial sandpainting. Still others will vary an element to make it visually more pleasing to the artist himself.

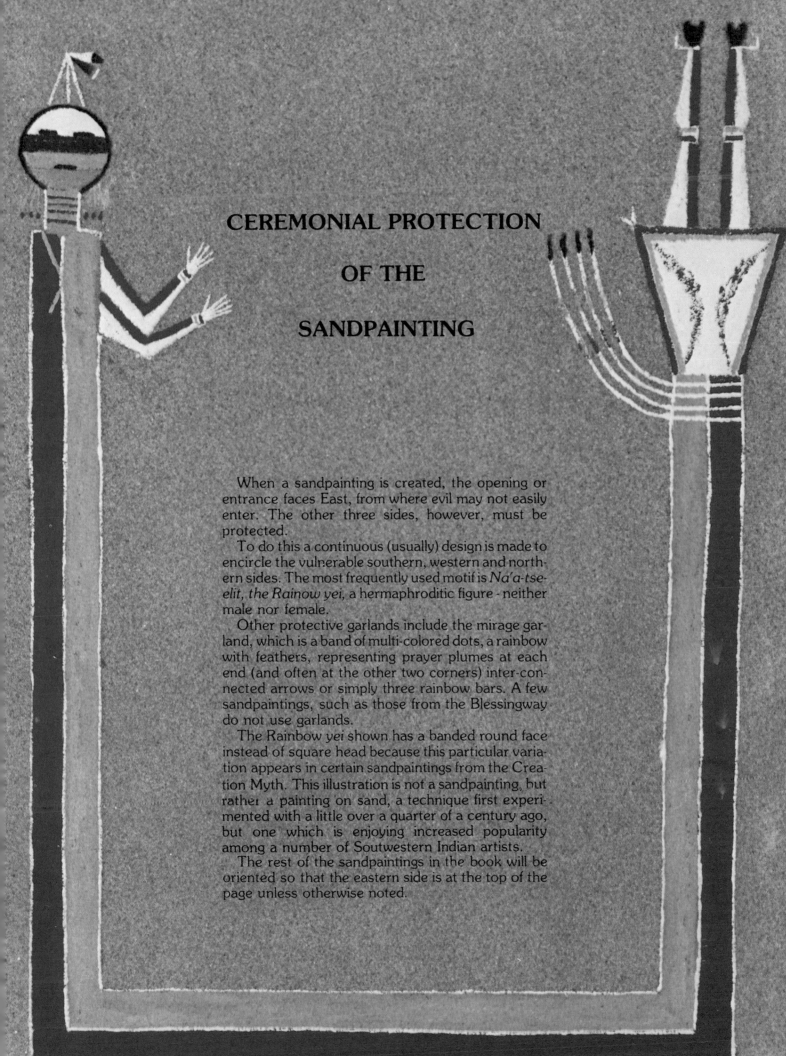

CEREMONIAL PROTECTION

OF THE

SANDPAINTING

When a sandpainting is created, the opening or entrance faces East, from where evil may not easily enter. The other three sides, however, must be protected.

To do this a continuous (usually) design is made to encircle the vulnerable southern, western and northern sides. The most frequently used motif is *Na'a-tse-elit, the Rainow yei,* a hermaphroditic figure - neither male nor female.

Other protective garlands include the mirage garland, which is a band of multi-colored dots, a rainbow with feathers, representing prayer plumes at each end (and often at the other two corners) inter-connected arrows or simply three rainbow bars. A few sandpaintings, such as those from the Blessingway do not use garlands.

The Rainbow *yei* shown has a banded round face instead of square head because this particular variation appears in certain sandpaintings from the Creation Myth. This illustration is not a sandpainting, but rather a painting on sand, a technique first experimented with a little over a quarter of a century ago, but one which is enjoying increased popularity among a number of Soutwestern Indian artists.

The rest of the sandpaintings in the book will be oriented so that the eastern side is at the top of the page unless otherwise noted.

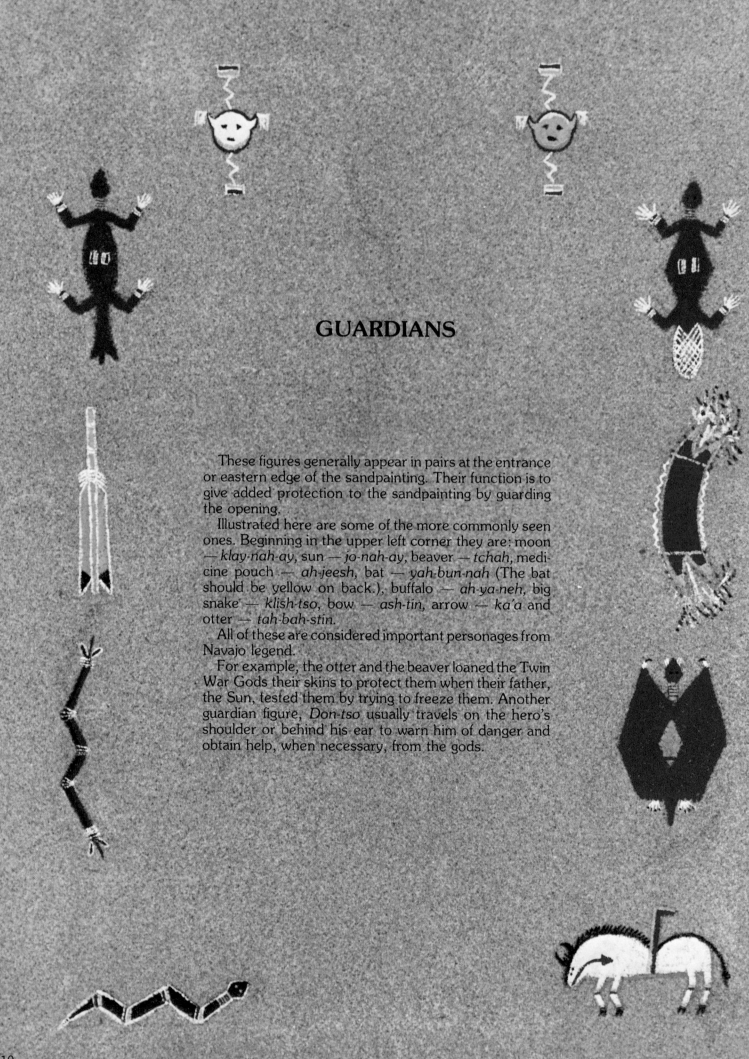

GUARDIANS

These figures generally appear in pairs at the entrance or eastern edge of the sandpainting. Their function is to give added protection to the sandpainting by guarding the opening.

Illustrated here are some of the more commonly seen ones. Beginning in the upper left corner they are: moon — *klay-nah-ay*, sun — *jo-nah-ay*, beaver — *tchah*, medicine pouch — *ah-jeesh*, bat — *yah-bun-nah* (The bat should be yellow on back.), buffalo — *ah-ya-neh*, big snake — *klish-tso*, bow — *ash-tin*, arrow — *ka'a* and otter — *tah-bah-stin*.

All of these are considered important personages from Navajo legend.

For example, the otter and the beaver loaned the Twin War Gods their skins to protect them when their father, the Sun, tested them by trying to freeze them. Another guardian figure, *Don-tso* usually travels on the hero's shoulder or behind his ear to warn him of danger and obtain help, when necessary, from the gods.

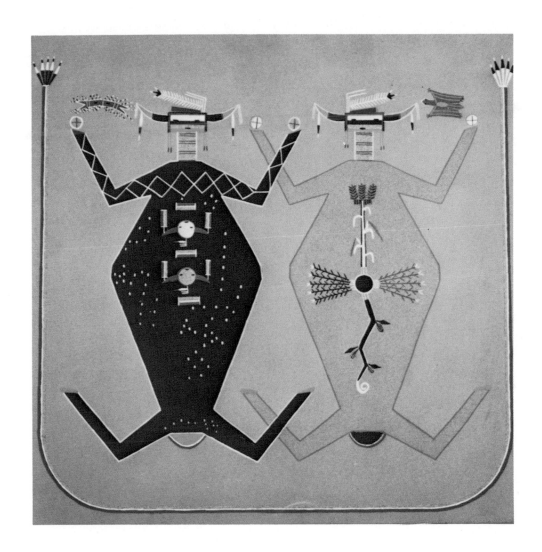

FATHER SKY AND MOTHER EARTH

Father Sky, *Yaah-diklith beh-hasteen,* and Mother Earth, *Nahas-tsan beh-assun,* appear in many sandpaintings throughout most of the Navajo Ways, including the Shooting Way, Mountain Way and Blessingway. They are invoked not because of a part in a particular story, but because of their strength and all-pervading importance.

Here they are accurately portrayed with banded rectangular faces and horns, symbolizing their power. (The figure in the lower right corner of page 21 shows the head that is more commonly, if somewhat incorrectly, used.) In the body of Mother Earth are the four sacred plants — corn, bean, squash and tobacco and in the body of Father Sky are the constellations, including the Milky Way represented by the intertwined zig-zag lines and the sun and the moon. The guardians are a medicine bag and the bat.

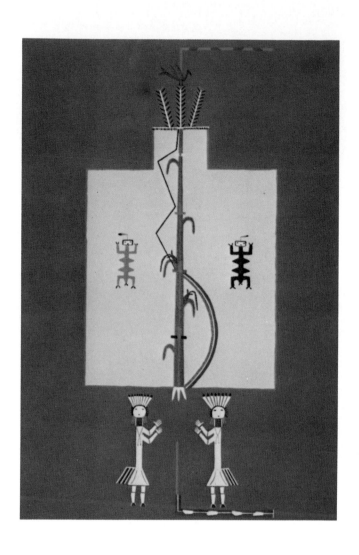

BLESSING WAY

Both of these sandpaintings are from a sequence that are used in the Blessing Way, or *Hozhoni*. This ceremony was once more important and longer, having now declined to a one to three day ritual. The one above was the fourth in a sequence, but is now the one most often used in the shorter observances.

The east, for this particular sandpainting, would be to the right rather than the top. The footprints on the rainbow represent the path of Man coming from one of the Underworld and passing between *Eth-kay-nah-ashi*, whose name translates as "Those-Who-Go-Together". They are twins created in the Second World by Begochiddy. The rainbow path changes to a yellow one, representing corn pollen.

The path continues up the corn, alongside the female rainbow and male lightning which carry it on up north to the yellow pollen footsteps. The two figures on either side of the corn are Big Fly.

COYOTE STEALING FIRE

Taken from an incident in the Creation Story, this sandpainting shows *Etsay-Hashkeh*, Coyote, stealing fire from the sleeping *Hashjesh-jin* or Fire God, who is shown holding a medicine bag in his left hand and a feather in his right where he should be holding a ring. The zig-zag lines running across his arms and shoulders represent the Milkway Way. The symbol beneath the medincine pouch is the fire.

The crosses represent various stars and constellations, with the red line indicating the trailing embers left by Coyote (also known to the Navajo as *Mah-ih* or He-who-wanders-about). It passes through the home of the Sun with its eagle guardian in the lower right corner and through the home of the Moon in the upper right to the upper left which is the home of First Man *(Etsay-hasteen)* and First Woman *(Etsay-Assun)*. The large circles in the upper and lower left represent hogans.

> I am the frivilous coyote—
> I wander about.
> I have seen Hasjesh-jin's fire—
> I wander about.
> I stole his fire from him—
> I wander about.
> I have it! I have it!
> from the Creation Chant

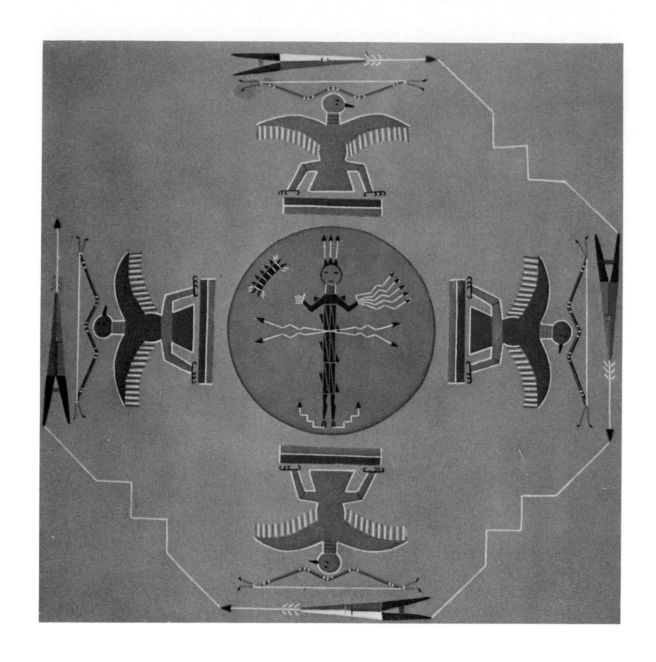

MONSTER SLAYER

Known as *Nayenezgani*, he is shown here standing against the sun, as he appears in the Female Shootingway. He is armed with crooked lightning, given to him by his father the Sun. *Nayenezgani's* brother, Born-of-Water *(Tobaschischin)* was given straight lightning. The serrated edges of his body indicate that he is wearing flint armor, also given to him by the Sun.

Around him are four eagles, each astride a rainbow bar which protects them, giving them greater power and strength. The sandpainting is protected by the bow guardians and a garland of arrows.

The two brothers, usually referred to as the Twin War Gods, are the focus of much of Navajo legend. They destroyed most of the terrible monsters or *Yei-tso* who inhabited the earth in its early days. (The great lava flow near Grants, New Mexico is believed to be the dried blood of one of these fearsome *Yei-tso*.) Among the few *Yei-tso* to survie were poverty, sickness and death.

B'ganaskiddy is known in English by a variety of names: Hump-backed *Yei*, Navajo God of Plenty or of Harvest and Camel God. The last name, which is completely absurd, probably was given by a trader who knew nothing of Navajo religion and when pressed for a name by a tourist, named it, based on the apparent hump on the back.

The hump is actually a deerskin bag, painted black. The short white stripes indicate the contents — seeds. The bag usually has five eagle plumes tied to it.

In his hands he is holding the strings of a medicine bag in the shape of a weasel. He may also be seen holding a netted water jug or a rod. This sandpainting correctly portrays him with Mountain Sheep horns, but many sandpainters fail to include the horns when portraying *B'ganaskiddy*.

B'GANASKIDDY

This unusual sandpainting is a double sandpainting from the Shooting Chant. The Navajo name for a double sandpainting translates as 'facing itself'.

On the left is Holy Man who went hunting with his brother, Holy Boy. Holy Man shot a Mountain Sheep, shown in the white oval near the top as a guardian-type figure, with an arrow, whose fletching was made of feathers from a bird he had stolen. He was captured by the Thunder People with their lightning bolts and taken up to the Sky People to be reprimanded and taught how to better use his power. Here we see Holy Man surrounded by Thunders and in the company of two guardians — Big Fly and Otter, whose skin had protected him from the lightning. Holy Man learned ceremonies to cure people who had illnesses caused by lightning and then left in search of his brother, Holy boy.

Holy Boy had gone in another direction and found a pool of water with a reed in the center. Attached to the reed were two eagle feathers. He tried to grab them three times and three times he missed. On the fourth time he fell into the water and was swallowed by a huge fish which took him down to the home of the Water People. The fish is represented at the four sides of Holy Boy, who is surrounded by a star, representing his being swallowed. The fish, while appearing much like a horned toad, is a fish, with the protrusions on the side being its fins and his forked tail shown as well.

In Holy Boy's right hand is the flint knife he used to cut his way out of the fish. In his right are the herbs he used to heal the wound in the fish. The corn plant at his side is not as much a part of the story as it is a part of the ceremony, in which the patient is given a medicine made of fish blood and corn pollen rolled into a little ball.

Also illustrated is one of the Thunders, who found Holy Boy, and a bear who helped look for him ad did the ducks and a wolf (looking more like a horse) who also participated in the search. The ducks should have rainbow loops at their bills and the ducks on two sides should have lightning.

The Water People were very angry at Big Fish for bringing an Earth person among them until Big Fly came and told them he was Holy Boy. When they learned this they taught him prayers, songs and sandpaintings to cure illnesses caused by water.

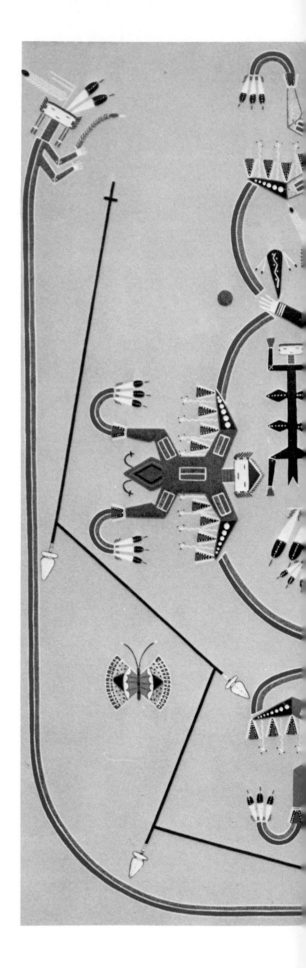

Holy Man Captured by the Thunders And Holy Boy Swallowed by a Fish

POLLEN BOY ON THE SUN

This sandpainting is often erroneously referred to as Eagle on the Sun, which is a complete misnomer since there is no such sandpainting.

Pollen Boy, called *Trahdah-de'en-eshki*, on the Sun or *Jo-honah-eh* appears in the Blessingway and may be used for two main purposes. If done with the four sacred plants (note that in this instance there appears to be two tobacco plants shown in two different colors rather than tobacco and beans) it is meant for a boy. If done for a man or a hunter, the plants would not be used. The feathers are colored for each direction, with nine feathers each and each feather representing a song from the ceremony. The sandpainting immediately to

the right is essentially the same, but is shown in the manner of a sunburst. The two items to each side of the sun are rattles. The sun should not be black for this particular sandpainting.

Still further to the right is Cornbug Girl or *Trahdah-de'en-atehd* on the Moon or *Klay-yo-nah-eh*. This sandpainting would be given for a woman. (Most chants, it should be noted, have female and male versions, with some varying slightly from the other, but with substantial changes in some.) Both Cornbug Girl and Corn Pollen Boy should be illustrated as solid colors with no second color outlining them.

SONG OF THE SUN CREATION

They emerged — they say he is planning it.
They emerged — they say he is planning it.
They emerged — they say he is planning it. . .
The sun will be created — they say he is planning it.
Its face will be blue — they say he is planning it.
Its eyes will be black — they say he is planning it.
Its chin will be yellow — they say he planning it. . . .
        —from the Creation Story

SONG OF THE MOON CREATION

They emerged — they say he is planning it.
They emerged — they say he is planning it.
They emerged — they say he is planning it. . .
The moon will be created — they say he is planning it.
Its face will be white — they say he is planning it.
Its chin will be yellow — they say he is planning it.
Its horns will be white — they say he is planning it. . .
        —from the Creation Story

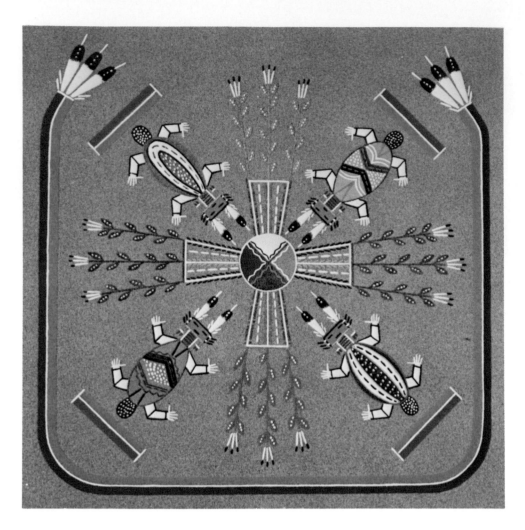

In another legend from the Creation Story, *Te-o-sol-hi's* child was stolen by Coyote. Enraged, *Te-o-sol-hi* began to flood the Third World, forcing everyone to flee up to the Fourth World. Still the waters came up after them. A conference was held and Coyote was found to be the culprit. As soon as he was made to return the child, the waters subsided.

The sandpainting below, with guardian figures in the background, is an example of a Navajo artist's individual interpretation of *Te-o-sol-hi*. The turquoise set in it, while adding interest visually, would not be regarded as an appropriate stone for this figure by traditional Navajo concepts.

WATER CREATURE

There was once a monster or *Yei-tso* whose name was *Tse-na-ye* or Travelling Rock, who would crush those who came near him. When Monster Slayer came to destroy him, *Tse-na-ye* hid on the bottom of a lake. Three times Monster Slayer tried to destroy him and three times *Tse-na-ye* hid. On the fourth time Monster Slayer spotted him under the water and struck him, shattering him into pieces and creating Water Creature, known also as *Te-o-sol-hi*. *Te-o-sol-hi* was instructed then to cause the rivers to flow and henceforth be responsible for them.

The figure in the lower right corner has basically the same intent, but reflects another Navajo artist's interpretation. The head used for this figure is often seen on Mother Earth-Father Sky sandpaintings and is generally recognized as being the Chirichuahua Apache version. (The Navajo and Apaache are both descended from the Athapascans and therefore have much in common.)

INTERPRETATIONS OF FATHER SKY AND MOTHER EARTH

These two figures are examples of variations and combinations of figures from traditional Navajo sandpainting that have come about, not because of inadvertent variations caused by a sandpainter who was unfamiliar with his culture and traditional sandpainting, but because of a conscious creative process based on intimate knowledge of Navajo religion. These reflect the artist's individual interpretation and experimentation with these forms.

In the figure in the upper left corner we have a yei-like figure standing between two solid bars as opposed to the rainbow bars that appear in traditional sandpaintings. The upper half of the torso is black and the figures in the lower half are those found in the body of Father Sky, but are done in the colors normally used for Mother Earth. Here both figures and the Navajo concept of balance have been metamorphosed into one.

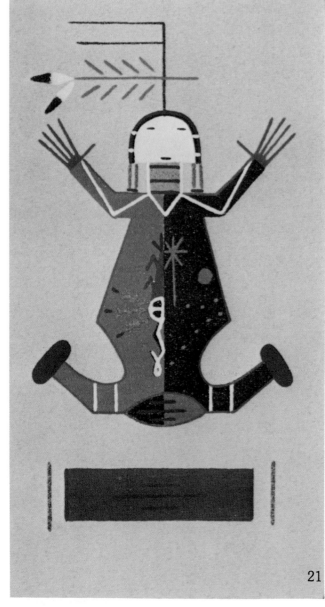

FROGS AND THE FOUR SACRED PLANTS

This sandpainting theme is a fundamental one that appears in a number of other sandpaintings, in whole or in part. The four sacred plants, beginning at the top right and going clockwise are: bean — *nah-othle,* corn — *nah-tah,* corn again appears in the third position where tobacco — *nah-toh* should be (it would look much like the bean plant but without the dots — see

page 31), and squash — *nah-yezzi.* The plants may be shown in plant or human form, but either way they are recognized as being the same and have the same name.

With the frogs included, this sandpainting would be used for treating a person who was crippled or suffering some form of paralysis, even arthritis. These types of illnesses are believed to be caused by the Water People.

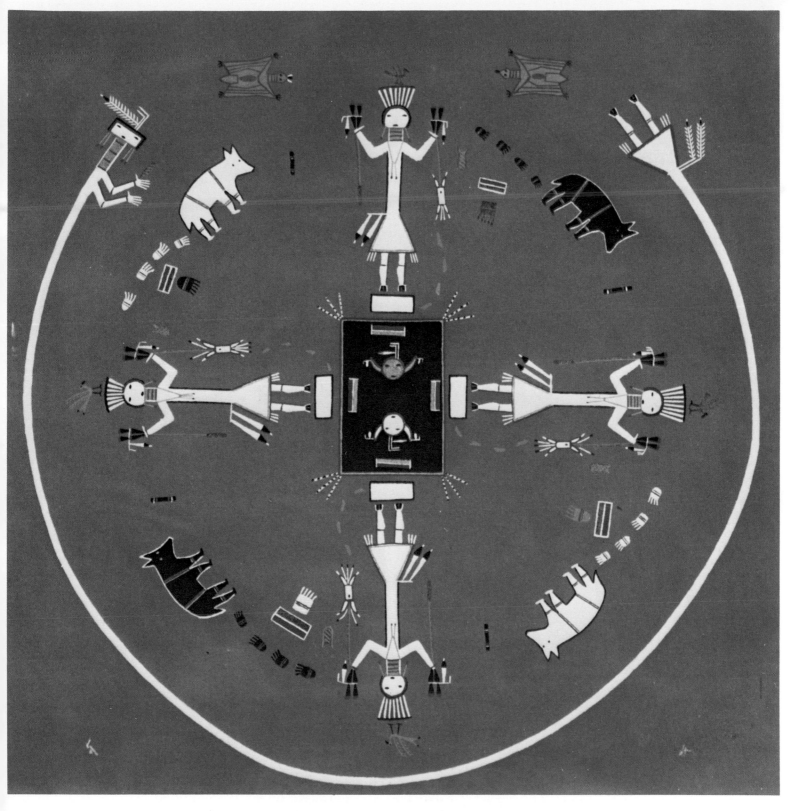

HOME OF THE BEARS

As mentioned on page 29, this story begins in the Blessing Way and continues in the Mountain Way. Bear Man is in pursuit of the maiden who fled from him. The tracks show his travels thus far and the bear paw with the rainbow bar indicates he is tracking her. The bar in front of each bear represents the pipe used to smoke the special tobacco which helped Bear Man eventually find her.

In the center are the sun and the moon and at the top are two bat guardians. Four *hastye-alt-yei* are shown holding a medicine bag in one hand and a bull-roarer in the other. He is usually referred to as Grandfather of the Gods or Talking God, though a more appropriate translation would be Speechless Talking One, for he is one of a small group who no longer speak as they once did in times long past. He also appears in the Nightway and had control over the dawn, corn and certain game animals. Of all the gods, he is regarded as being the most compassionate.

I, I am Talking God — now I wander about.

From under the East I wander about — now I wander about

The dawn lies toward me, I wander about — now I wander about

The white corn lies toward me — now I wander about . .

Before me, it is beautiful — it shows my way.

Behind me, it is beautiful — it shows my way.

NIGHT SKIES

This sandpainting is from the *N'tlo-he* or Hail Way, which is no longer performed, for no medicine man is alive who knows it. The last medicine man to perform it was Hasteen Klah, who knew an incredible total of six Ways. Fortunately Klah had the foresight to see that most of the ceremony was recorded.

In this we see the heads of figures on both sides holding up the night. The white line around the edge represents the dawn. In the body are the various constellations, which were placed in the sky by *Hasje-hasjin*. Among them is *No-ho-kos*, known in English as the Big Dipper. The intertwined zig-zag lines are the Milky Way. Around the edges, top and bottom, are a number of guardians, including yellow male and blue female eagles, the antelope and the bat, messenger of the night, who is shown here on a bed of corn pollen.

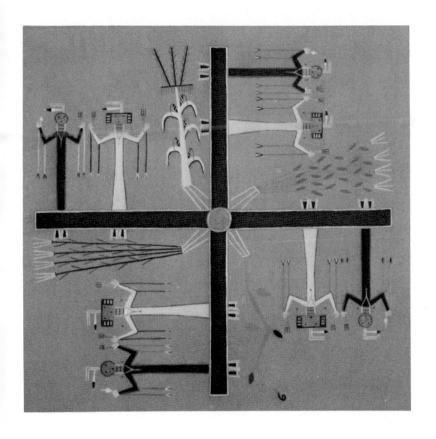

When he finally reaches the lake that is his destination, the gods catch his log and help him to shore. In the sandpainting at the right we see them: clockwise from the top they are Talking God, *B'ganaskiddy*, Talking God and *Hastye-o-gahn*, whose name is not translatable.

Wandering about on land the hero comes upon a whirling cross with two *yeis* seated on each end. From them he learns the knowledge of farming and is given seeds. He then returns home to share these gifts with his people.

Figures in Navajo sandpaintings generally proceed sunrise or clockwise, for this reason: The log in the sandpainting in the lower right corner should have the *yeis* on the opposite side, as in the one on the upper left.

WHIRLING LOGS

The Whirling Log or *Tsil-ol-ni* story occurs in both the Night and the Feather or Plume Way. The hero of the story sets out on a long journey. At first the gods try to persuade him against going, but seeing his determination, help him hollow out a log in which he will travel down the river.

Along the way he has many misadventures which ultimately reslult in his gaining important ceremonial knowledge. In one such instance he and his craft are captured by the Water People who carry him down beneath the waters to the home of Water Monster. Black God threatens to set fire to Water Monster's home and the hero is released, but not before being taught by Frog how to cure the illnesses caused by the Water People.

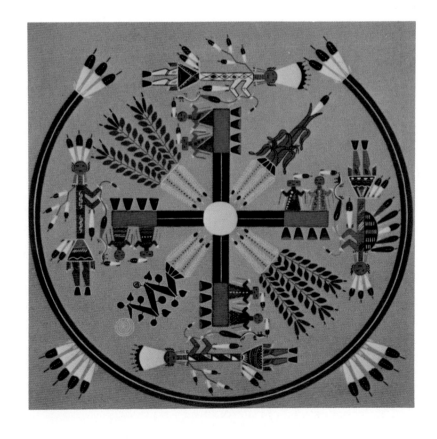

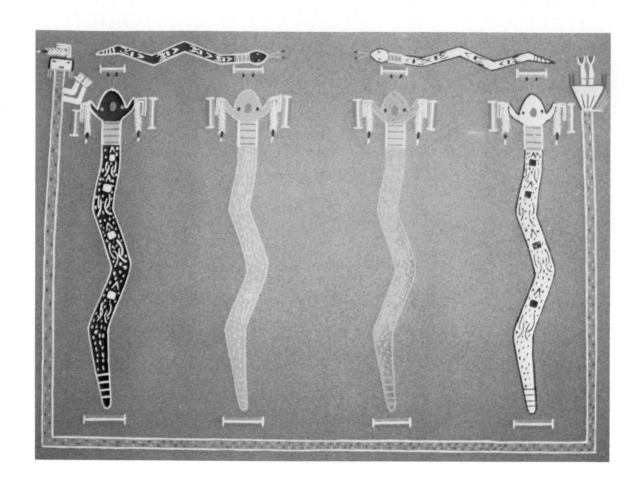

SNAKES

Snakes, because of their shape and speed have long been associated with lightning by the Navajo. Both are feared because of their great power. At the top is a sandpainting of the Snake People. The yellow fangs indicate that they are not poisonous.

The sandpainting at the right is of Endless Snake, known as *Klish-do-nuhti'i*. He is poisonous here, as shown by his red fangs. The snake appears in a variety of Ways, including the Beauty Way, Big Star Way, Wind Way and Shooting Way.

In one story the hero uses poisonous tobacco to overcome Big Snake Man and render him unconscious. Big Snake's wife pleads with the hero to restore her husband, in exchange for all their valuables. After the hero does this he trades the valuables back to Big Snake for the sandpaintings and ceremonial knowledge he had come seeking in the first place.

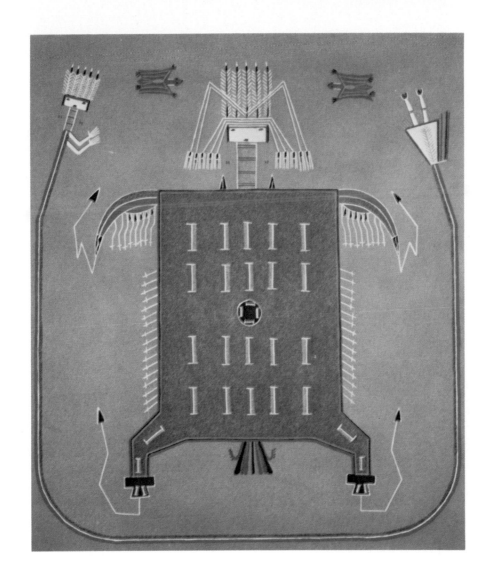

THUNDER

The Thunder People are very powerful and therefore potentially dangerous gods. Above is shown *Ikne'etso* or Big Thunder with *ikne'e-ka'a*, lightning, coming from his wings and feet. He should not be confused with the thunderbird, who is not a part of Navajo religion. The many rainbow bars show his great strength. Above his head are two bat guardians, messengers for the Night. The elaborate weasel headdresses show that this sandpainting was done for the Mountain Chant.

The figure on the right is a more commonly seen representation of the Thunder People.

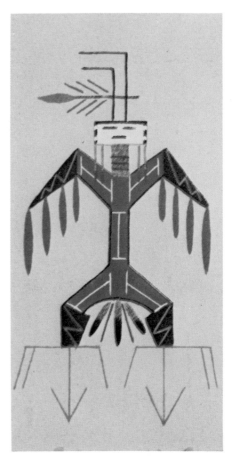

SAND DUNE MONSTER

This sandpainting is from the ceremony called "The Two Who Went to Their Father", which is the chronicle of the journey of the Twin War Gods who undertook to visit their father, the Sun, and the many tests he put them through before granting them the weapons they needed to dispatch the monsters or *Yei-tso* who used to inhabit the earth.

Depicted here is Sand Dune Monster, who trapped and killed unwary travellers with his shifting sands. The Twin War Gods, represented here by two crosses, travelled over this danger on a rainbow which had been given them by Spider Woman.

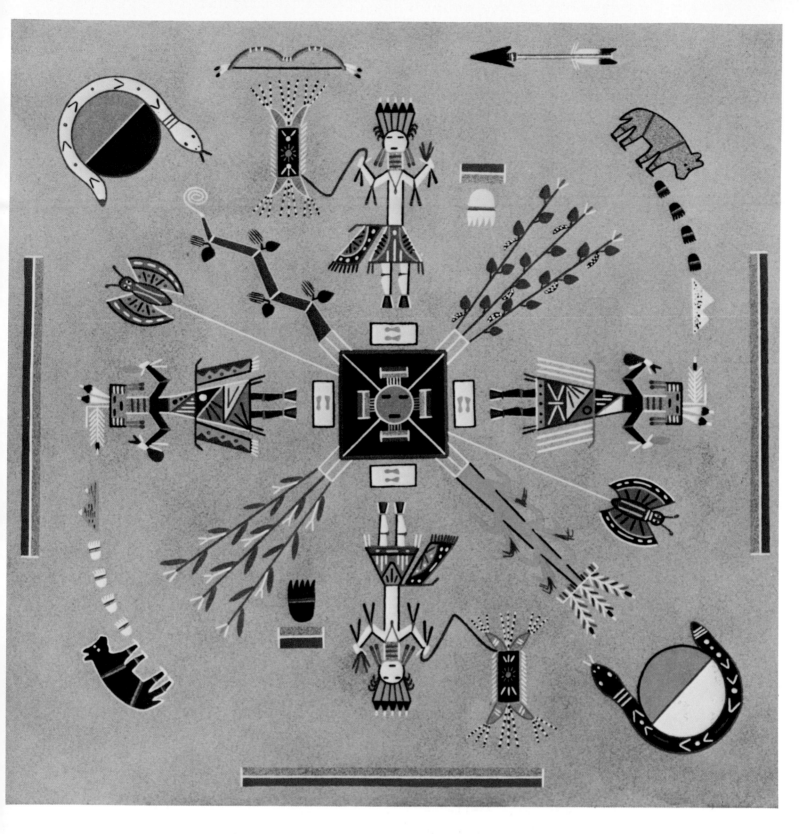

HOME OF THE BEAR AND THE SNAKE

This sandpainting theme occurs in both the Beauty Way and the Mountain Way, but it has its origins in yet another — the Blessing Way.

Big Snake Man and Bear Man, disguised as very old men compete successfully in a battle against the Pueblo people and in successive archery contests against Monster Slayer and his companions for the possession of two beautiful maidens who are here illustrated as the two square-headed female figures at the right and left. Though the two old men win every contest Monster Slayer can think of, they are still denied their prizes.

That night, while the others attended a social dance, Big Snake Man and Bear Man transformed themselves into handsome rich young men. Using a sweet-smelling magic tobacco, they lure the girls to them. Upon awakening in the morning the maidens find that the young men have changed into the old men they had spurned the day before. Frightened, they flee.

Big Snake's Man's pursuit of one of the maidens continues in the Beauty Way, while Bear Man's chase is a part of the Mountain Way.

The butterflies symbolize the beauty of the maidens and the bear tracks the following of their pursuers. The snakes are shown in their hogans and the bears near their mountain homes. The two figures at the top and bottom are both *Hastye-alt-yei* or Talking God.

29

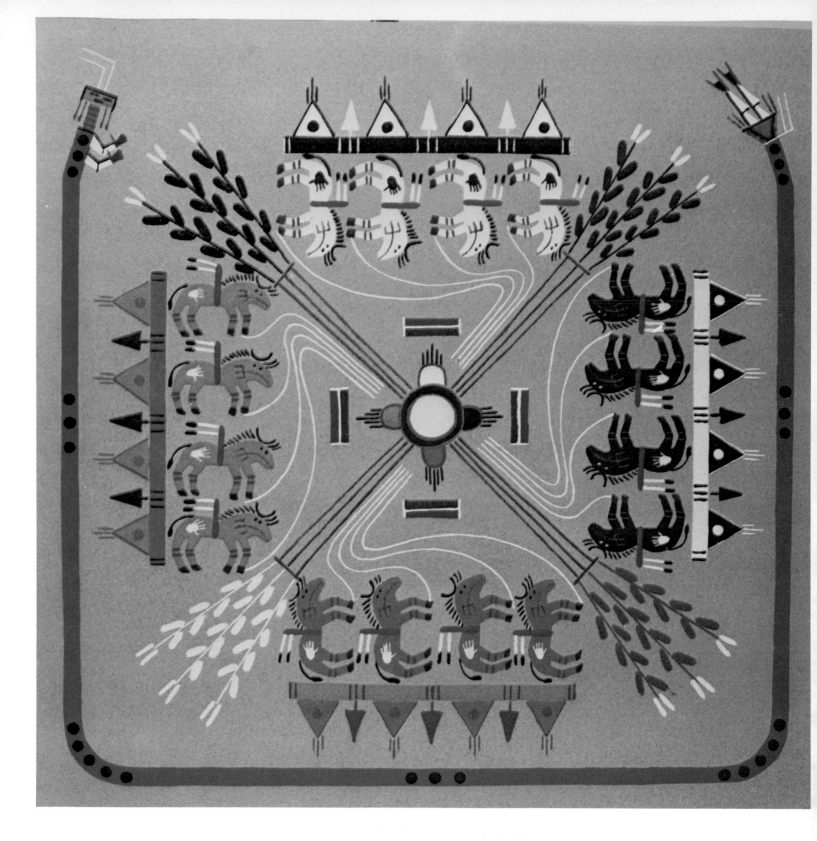

THE BUFFALO PEOPLE

This sandpainting is often referred to by the name "The Buffalo Who Never Die". This title came from a story of a man who married the daughter of the chief of the *Ah-yah-neh* or Buffalo People. When the Buffalo People left to return to their home on the Plains of the East, he was told not to follow them.

He did follow them and when discovered, the Buffalo People decided to kill him. Prepared for this he armed himself with special magic given him by the gods and killed all the Buffalo People instead. He eventually revived them in exchange for certain ceremonial knowledge which they had. The red lines on the Buffalo People in this sandpainting should be red and blue rainbows instead, which symbolize the fact that they have been brought back to life. Also the white hands on the buffalo do not appear in traditional representations of the Buffalo People. The tipis in the sandpainting represent the home of the Buffalo People. The white lines represent their trails to the water.

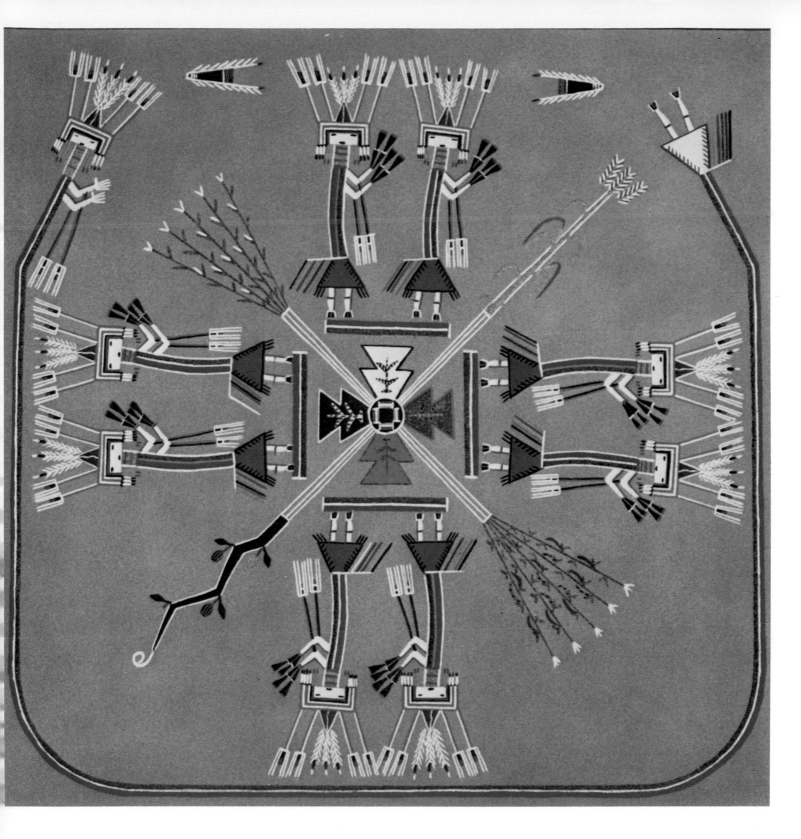

RAINBOW PEOPLE

These are the Rainbow People or *Na'a-tse-elit yei* as they appear in the Mountain Way, with the elaborate weasel headdresses. The Rainbow People usually appear in pairs much as one often sees double rainbows in nature. They hold double rattles that are characteristic of the Mountain Way. The four sacred plants are present because of their association with water and the two guardians are medicine pouches.

Adjacent to the Emergence center and the holy water (the black circle outlined in white with rainbow bars to increase its holiness and strength) are four cloud symbols, each colored for the four different directions. On each of the cloud symbols are dragonflys, who are the messengers of the sun. Here, expressed symbolically, you have the origin, both in legend and in fact, of the rainbow with the cloud symbols and the dragonflys representing the combination of moisture and light that brings about the rainbow.

SUGGESTED READING

Bahti, Tom. Southwestern Indian Ceremonials. K.C. Publications, Las Vegas, Nevada. 1970.

Foster, Kenneth E. Navajo Sandpaintings. Navajo Tribal Museum, Window Rock, Arizona. 1964.

Newcomb, Franc J. and Gladys Reichard. Sandpaintings of the Navajo Shooting Chant. Dover Publications, New York. Republished 1975.

Reichard, Gladys A. Navajo Medicine Man Sandpaintings. Revised edition. Dover Publications, New York, 1977.

Wyman, Leland C. Mountainway of the Navajo. University of Arizona Press, Tucson. 1975.

Wyman, Leland C. Navaho Sandpainting; The Huckel Collection. Taylor Museum, Colorado Springs. 1964.

The world before me is restored in beauty
The world behind me is restored in beauty
The world above me is restored in beauty
The world below me is restored in beauty
All things around me are restored in beauty
It is finished in beauty
It is finished in beauty
It is finished in beauty
It is finished in beauty.

INSIDE BACK COVER

"Sun Rise of Beauty" by Baatsoslanii — A beginning of harmony for the plants and the creatures who live among them. The bear is the guardian symbol.

BACK COVER

These four figures, each a different color to represent the four directions, are the Nil-tsi yei, or wind people. In one hand they hold cloud symbols and in the other they hold the feather that is used to create the winds. The Wind People are very important in Navajo legend for it was they who relayed the ceremonial knowledge given by the Holy People to the Navajo.